SEPTEMBER
TO SEPTEMBER

Poems for All Year Round

*A Collection of Original Poems
Especially Designed for Classroom Use*

Dee Lillegard

CHILDRENS PRESS ®

CHICAGO

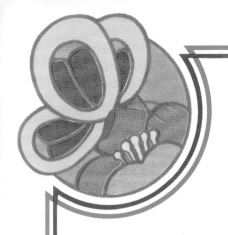

Editor: Beatrice Beckman

Designer: Karen Yops

Artist: Yoshi Miyake

Acknowledgments

Grateful acknowledgment is made to the publishers and copyright holders for permission to use the following poems in this book:

"All Aboard," used by permission of the FRIEND magazine.

"Being the Best You Can Be," from WEE WISDOM, June-July 1981.

"By Any Name, I'm Still the Same," from WEE WISDOM, February 1976.

"Caterpillar," from WEE WISDOM, June-July 1985.

"A Gift for Mother," from WEE WISDOM, May 1979.

"Have A Ball," from CHILDREN'S PLAYMATE, April 1979, by Benjamin Franklin Literary and Medical Society, Inc., Indianapolis. Reprinted by permission of the publisher.

"Hear Me," from WEE WISDOM, March 1981.

"If You Want to Be a Cowboy," from JACK AND JILL, August-September 1975, by The Saturday Evening Post Company, Indianapolis. Reprinted by permission of the publisher.

"The Kettle Town Five," from WEE WISDOM, March 1975.

"Look Both Ways," from HUMPTY DUMPTY'S MAGAZINE, August-September 1984, by Benjamin Franklin Literary and Medical Society, Inc., Indianapolis. Reprinted by permission of the publisher.

"Love Is. . ." from WEE WISDOM, February 1986.

"Many Kinds of Christmas," originally appeared as "Christmas Around the World" in JACK AND JILL, December 1979, Benjamin Franklin Literary and Medical Society, Inc., Indianapolis. Reprinted by permission of the publisher.

"Nice and New," adapted from STORY FRIENDS, September 4, 1977 and September 1, 1985.

"A Peanut Butter Poem," from EXPLORE, July 25, 1976.

"The Perfect Pet," from WEE WISDOM, April 1976.

"A Space Trip," from WEE WISDOM, November 1980.

"Thank You," from WEE WISDOM, November 1985.

"Walking in the Snow," from CHILDREN'S PLAYMATE, January 1976, by The Saturday Evening Post Company, Indianapolis. Reprinted by permission of the publisher.

"Wendell's Goat," from WEE WISDOM, April 1976.

"Whale and I," from HUMPTY DUMPTY'S MAGAZINE, May 1979, by Parents' Enterprises, Inc. Reprinted by permission of the publisher.

"What Do They Do?" from WEE WISDOM, October 1980.

"Where Is Love?" from WEE WISDOM, February 1981.

"Yankee Doodle Dandy," from JACK AND JILL, June-July 1977.

Lillegard, Dee.
  September to September.

  (A Teacher's resource book)
  Includes index.
  Summary: A collection of poems organized month by
month around typical themes presented in preschool,
kindergarten, and the early grades, with suggestions
for singing to familiar tunes or using with various
classroom activities.
  1. Children's poetry, American. [1. American
poetry] I. Title. II. Series.
PS3562.I4557S4 1986   811'.54   86-13622
ISBN 0-516-03297-6

For Mom, my first teacher. . .

**and for April and Camellia,
Collin and Brett**

Introduction

The poems in this collection were many years in the making. Originally created for the children in my life—and the child in myself—they sprang into being from sheer joy and were shaped by my love and respect for the English language. They are meant to be read aloud with lively rhythm and expression, to be heard and shared.

Children experience spontaneous pleasure and a sense of inner unity through rhythm and rhyme. They have a natural poetic sense that should be encouraged as early as possible. Hearing poetry may inspire them to create poems of their own. Ideally, an adult or an older child should write down these original creations as they occur. In this way we can affirm in the children their own creativity and the value of their individual perspectives, while teaching them that poetry is a vital part of themselves and the world around them.

It is my hope that, through your voice, the poems in this collection will spring to life from the printed page. I thank you for your part in recreating them. And I especially want to thank Nancy Hubbard Johnson, children's librarian and special friend, for her inspiration and encouragement.

Dee Lillegard

Contents

SEPTEMBER

Look Both Ways

I never run across the street—
I always stop to see
If something big is coming in
The direction of *me*.

You never know—
There might be cars.
There also might be
DINOSAURS!

And what if one
Should step on me!
That's why I always
Stop to see.

The First-Day Game*

The first day of school
There are lots of new faces.
The first day of school
There are new things and places—

Corners to peek in
And pictures to see,
Things I can touch
And new things that touch me.

But the first day of school
My favorite game
Is What shining face
Goes with each different name?

*See teacher's note 1.

The Clap and Quiet Poem

Clap clap clap. . .	*(Leader claps)*
My hands make noise.	
Clap clap clap. . .	
Let's hear the boys.	
Clap clap clap. . .	*(Boys join in)*
Now girls clap too.	
Clap clap clap. . .	*(Girls join in)*
And now we're through!	
Quiet hands.	*(Whisper—show hands)*
Quiet face.	*(Hands to the face)*
Let's have quiet	*(Forefinger to the lips)*
Every place.	
Shhh. . .	

Hands*

Hands are for washing
Before you can eat.
Hands are for making
Your room nice and neat.

Hands are for holding
The person you love.
Hands are for warming
In mittens or gloves.

Hands can do magic—
They build and they make
Houses and airplanes
And pictures and cake!

*See teacher's note 2.

Say Please

Look up! Look down!
Look all around.

Open your eyes.
Close your eyes.
Open your eyes.
Close your eyes.

Now you're sleeping
In your bed.
Wake up!
And rub your head!

Touch your nose.
Touch your toes.
Rub your knees.
Say *please*!

Do what the poem says.

Getting Dressed

My buttons won't button.
My snaps won't snap.
All I can wear
Is my baseball cap!

*What will people say
When they see you that way?*
"Good morning—My goodness!
Well, have a nice day—"

*What do you think people would say if you
went outside with nothing on but a cap?*

Crayons*

Sticks of color—
Orange, red,
Yellow, green,
And brown like bread.

Blue like water
In the sea.
Purple like bruises
On my knee.

Black like night
When I'm in bed,
Dreaming in yellow,
Orange, and red.

Do you remember your dreams?
Do you dream in color?
Maybe you could draw your
dreams in color.

*May be sung to the tune of ''Baa Baa Black Sheep''

Scissors and Shapes*

Snip, snip—circle!
Snip, snip—square!
Snip go my scissors
Everywhere!

Snip, snip—rectangle,
Triangle, too.
I'm going to have a lot of shapes
When I get through!

*See teacher's note 3.

Pasting

A little dab here—
A little dab there—
Be careful—don't let it
Stick to your hair!

A little dab—there—
Not too thick—
Now put it on the paper
Where you want it to stick.

Painting*

Swish swash brown.
Swish swash blue.
I love to paint!
It's my favorite thing to do.

A little green for grass
And some yellow for a sun.
Another swish swash—there's a tree
And I'm done!

Do you like it?

*See teacher's note 4.

The Seasons

Spring,
Summer,
Autumn (which
we also call
Fall),
and finally
Winter.
That's all
the seasons.

Spring,
Summer,
Autumn
(or Fall),
Then Winter.
That's all.
The seasons are four.
There are no more.

How many seasons are there?
Raise a finger for each one as it is named in the poem.
Remember, autumn and fall are different
names for the same season.

What Falls
in the Fall?

In the fall
Do you fall out of bed?
In the fall
Do you land on your head?

In the fall
Do houses fall down?
And buildings and butterflies
All over town?

Something must fall
In the fall, if you please.
Oh yes! The leaves fall.
They fall from the trees!

It's Autumn!*

The leaves turn yellow.
The leaves turn brown.
The leaves turn red
And they
   all
      fall
         down!

The leaves turn yellow.
The leaves turn red.
They all fall down
On top of my head!

*May be sung to the tune of "The Mulberry Bush"

My Secret*

I'm holding a secret
Here in my hand.
It's little as a bug,
But it's going to be grand.

Do you think you can guess
The secret I've got?
It's smooth as a baby,
And it's quiet as a thought.

Oh, I've got a seed,
If you really want to know.
I'll set it in the ground
And it will grow and GROW and GROW!

*May be sung to the tune of "The Farmer in the Dell"

If There Weren't Any Seeds

If there weren't any seeds,
   there would be no trees,
   no apples, no beans, no corn, no peas.
If there weren't any seeds,
   there would be no wheat—
   no bread or biscuits for us to eat.
If there weren't any seeds,
   how could anything be?
   No flowers, no lovely things to see,
   no grass on the ground,
   not a daisy around,
   not even weeds—
If there weren't any seeds. . .

Do you think we need seeds?

OCTOBER

Trees*

Some have needles, but not for sewing.
Some have cones, but not ice cream.
Some just keep on growing and growing,
While some seem to be dreaming a dream.

Some give syrup, some give fruit
Like peaches, pears, and cherries.
Some have squirrels and owls that hoot,
And some. . . I think. . . have fairies.

*See teacher's note 5.

In the Apple Tree

Bluebird lives in the apple tree.
She sings sweetly down to me.
She tells me of her cozy nest
In the hole in the tree that she loves best.

She tells me that her bluebird mate
And she herself can hardly wait—
They have bluebird eggs, you see,
That soon will be their family.

They'll live together in their cozy nest
In the hole in the tree that they love best.
Happy in her apple tree,
Bluebird sings her news to me!

High and Low

Stand on your tippy-toes.   *(Stretching, reaching)*
Stretch with me
For pears and apricots
Up in the tree.

Bend down low. . .   *(Bending down and grabbing)*
You'll have to stoop
For squash and cabbage
To put in the soup.

An orange orange,   *(Stretching, reaching)*
A golden peach,
Shiny red apples
Too high to reach. . .

Now let's go digging.   *(Bending down and digging)*
Look what I've found!
Potatoes and carrots   *(Standing up straight,*
Asleep in the ground!   *"holding" potatoes*
   and carrots)

A Peanut-Butter Poem

Peanut butter and jelly.
Peanut butter and jam.
A peanut-butter person,
That's what I am.

Peanut butter on white bread.
Peanut butter on brown.
Peanut butter right side up
Or upside down.

P. B. and butter.
P. B. and marmalade.
I love P. B. and anything!
That's how I was made.

What is P.B.?
Are you a peanut-butter person?

The Great Fruit and Vegetable Fight

BETTY BEET says, "I'm better than any old banana."
BARNEY BANANA says, "Who needs a beet!"
COLLIN THE CARROT says, "I'm stronger than an apricot."
ALLISON APRICOT says, "You're no treat!"

GARY GREEN BEANS says, "I'm full of vitamins."
GLORIA GRAPES says, "I'm not impressed."
SARA SQUASH says, "Vegetables are everything!"
PEGGY PEACH says, "Fruits are best!"

TOMMY TOMATO says, "What's all this fighting?
   Don't you fellows know?
   Boys and girls need fruits *and* vegetables
   In order to grow."

PATSY PEAR says, "Let's be friends."
PETE POTATO says, "Not with *your* group.
   Go jump in the jello!" "Well!" says PATSY,
   "You can go jump in the soup!"

"Come on," say THE KIDS. "Stop fighting.
   We don't care if you're big or small.
   If you will just be good for us,
   We'll love you one and all!"

Knife, Fork, and Spoon*

This is my knife.
It cuts my meat
In little pieces
Just right to eat.

(Forefinger sawing the palm of opposite hand)

This is the fork.
It pokes my meat
And picks it up
For me to eat.

(Three fingers poking the palm and moving to the mouth)

This is my spoon.
It carries my peas
So they don't fall down
All over my knees!

(Cupped hand, with fingers wiggling like peas in the spoon)

*May be sung to the tune of ''Twinkle Twinkle Little Star''

When Mother Washes Our Hair

Ooh, shampoo!
It gets in our eyes.
When it does,
My sister cries.

When Mother really
Scrubs her scalp,
My sister hollers,
"Help! Help!"

She doesn't like
The suds and foam.
She doesn't care
For brush and comb.

If Sister had her way,
I guess
Her head would be
An awful mess!

Hands in the Basin

Ten little people
Going for a swim.
Jump in!
Wiggle all around.
All squeeze together
With the soap I've found.

(Fingers dangling, wiggling in front)
(Hands up, diving in)
(Fingers wiggling together)
(Fingers clasped)

Ten little people
Washing up for lunch.
All scrub together
In a slippery,
Soapy
Bunch.

(Washing hands vigorously)

Don't splash!

(Washing slows down and stops)

Tooth Beast*

Teeth can't talk,
But if they could,
I know what they would say:
"If you can and if you would,
Brush us every day—
At least two times and better, three—
We'd be as good as we could be
And try to stay
As white as chalk."

If teeth could talk
They'd surely say:
"Please help us fight that beast
DECAY."
And I'd be happy at the least
To keep that awful beast
AWAY!

*See teacher's note 6.

Bath Time*

Did you ever hear a tree say,
"I don't want. . . I don't want. . . "
Did you ever hear a tree say,
"I don't want a bath!"

But the rain pours
And the wind scrubs
And the whole yard
Is a bathtub.

Did you ever hear a tree say,
"I don't want a bath!"

*May be sung to the tune of "Did You Ever See A Lassie?"

Christopher Columbus*

Sailing, sailing,
  Over the sea
In three little ships—
  One, two, three.

Land! Land!
  Land in view!
In fourteen-hundred
  And ninety-two.

We stand on America,
  Smiling in the sun.
Christopher Columbus,
  You are the one!

*See teacher's note 7.

It's Halloween

Watch out! A witch!
Black cat! Take care!
Skeletons, ghosts, and pirates!
Beware!

They're coming here.
They're coming soon.
I saw them under
The orange moon!

They're coming here
To give us a fright.
Well, let them come.
It's Halloween night!

Pretending*

I have a key, a secret key.
It opens every door
Of every place I want to be
And then a dozen more.

A room inside a castle,
Or a room made out of rock,
A room with monsters in it—
I don't even have to knock!

If you had a secret key, what door would
you open?
What do you think you would find?
*See teacher's note 8.

The Queen[*]

Q is for *quiet*.
   (You have to be quiet.
   It's fun if you try it.)
Shh! Quiet!

Q is for *quickly*.
   (You have to come quickly.
   No time to be tickly.)
Quiet! Come quickly!

Q is for *queen*.
   (You must see the queen.
   She's old, but not mean.)
Quiet! Quickly! The queen!

[*]See teacher's note 10.

The Costume Song[*]

The queen went out of the kingdom,
The queen went out of the kingdom,
The queen went out of the kingdom
   To see what she could see.

The ghost flew out of the castle,   *(3 times)*
   To see what he could see.

The pirate sailed over the seas,   *(3 times)*
   To see what he could see.

The monster came over the mountain,   *(3 times)*
   To see what he could see.

Now everyone else is going,   *(3 times)*
   To see what they can see.
   And there's nobody left but *me!*   *(Leader says)*

[*]May be sung to the tune of "The Bear Went Over the Mountain"
(see also teacher's note 9).

NOVEMBER

Myself

Two arms, two legs,   *(Fold arms, tap legs)*
One head, one nose.   *(Tap head, touch nose)*
Two hands, two feet,   *(Clap hands, stamp feet)*
Ten fingers, ten toes.   *(Wiggle fingers, stand on tiptoe)*

Two ears to hear,   *(Flap earlobes with fingers)*
Two eyes to see.   *(Blink eyes)*
Lots and lots of hair,   *(Muss up hair)*
But only one *me!*   *(Raise forefinger and point to self)*

The Yawn

Oh, what a yawn! What a big yawn!
Such a fine yawn that I put it in a sack.
I wanted to save it.
I don't know who gave it
To me, but it's mine and I wanted it back.
I *couldn't* let such a big yawn get away.
I might have to have it for some other day.

Try this with a puppet that can really yawn.
Can you save a yawn? Have you ever tried?
What is a yawn?

Listen

Listen!
Quiet!
What do I hear?
A mother doe
And her baby deer!

See them standing
Between the trees?
Don't scare them off.
Don't laugh!
Don't sneeze!

The Chair Over There*

Was there a bear
in the chair
over there?
  No. . .
Was there a pear
in the chair
over there?
  No. . .
What was in the chair?
Was it someone's underwear?
Who can tell me what was in the chair
over there?

*See teacher's note 11.

Dot to Dot

One, two, three—
Dot to dot.
It's a picture of something—
I wonder what.

Draw a line
From four to five.
Watch the picture
Come alive.

Six and seven,
Eight and nine—
Add another
Nice straight line

To ten and eleven.
What can it be?
Draw dot to dot
And soon you'll see.

Two Clocks

I have a clock all my own.
It ticks the time for me
With hands that go around and around,
One o'clock, two o'clock, three. . .

I have a clock all my own.
It *shines* the time for me
In numbers that I know so well,
One-0-0, two-0-0, three. . .

What kinds of clocks are we talking about?
How are they different?
What is the same about them?

Puzzle

A puzzle grows
piece by piece,
very slowly
filling space
as if too shy
to show its face.

Do you ever feel shy?
Do you know someone who is shy?
Is he or she kind of like
a puzzle to you?

Two Houses

My daytime house and nighttime house
Are not the same at all.
It's different when the sun comes up
And when the shadows fall.

My room is sometimes golden.
My room is sometimes black.
But when the sunshine goes away,
I know it will come back.

Do you really have two houses? It's the same house,
isn't it? Why does your room look so different at
different times of the night and day?

29

Surprise

I open the door
And I holler, "Hi!
I guess you're baking
A pumpkin pie!"

"How did you know?"
My mother replies.
"I thought it was going
To be a surprise.

"Did a little bird tell?
Or do you suppose
You figured it out
With your clever nose?"

I ask myself,
Did a little bird tell?
On no. . . it was just
That wonderful smell!

*Do you ever notice how the house
smells when someone is cooking?
What smells do you like a lot?
What smells do you not like?*

My Favorite Apples*

Some apples are red,
Some yellow, some green.
And some of them shine
When you polish them clean.

Some apples are juicy,
Some tart and some sweet.
But the ones in the pie
Are what *I* like to eat!

**See teacher's note 12.*

Harvest

Plant a seed.
Watch it grow.
Many seeds—
All in a row.

Watch the pumpkins
On the vine
Get so golden,
Fat and fine.

Watch the squashes
That appear.
See the corn
Come ear by ear.

When the harvest
Time arrives,
Watch the busy
Husbands, wives

Gather up
The crop with joy,
Helped by every
Girl and boy.

Plant a seed
And soon you'll know
Why the Pilgrims
Thanked God so.

Nights in a Tepee

If we lived in a tepee, round and tall,
A group of our people, big and small,
Would gather around a glowing fire,
Watching the flames grow higher and higher.

We'd listen to the wise man tell
Stories that cast a magic spell—
Tales of our brave and clever tribe,
Adventures too scary to describe.

For hours we'd watch the fire dance—
Hear the wise man's rhythmic chants.
I'd stay awake till he was through
If I were an Indian. Wouldn't you?

The Pilgrims Were People

The Pilgrims were people
Just like us.
But they had no cars
And they had no bus—

No grocery store,
No laundromat,
No television—
No, nothing like that!

The Pilgrims were people
Who built their own houses,
And made what they needed—
From candles to blouses—

And prayed to God
And made some more
Of what *you* can buy
At somebody's store!

Candle Song

Dip the candles—
Shape the candles—
All around the wick.
All about us
Night is falling,
Deep and dark and thick.

Dip the candles—
Shape the candles—
Light the candlelight.
Watch the candles
Melt—the candles
Make the cabin bright!

Two Little Words*

Two little words
That shine like the sun—
When someone says "Thank you"
For something you've done.

Two little words
That shine like a star—
When someone says "Thank you"
For what you are.

*May be sung to the tune of "Little Boy Blue"

Thank You

Thank you, sky, for bringing clouds.
Thank you, clouds, for bringing rain.
Thank you, rain, for feeding earth.
Thank you, earth, for giving grain.

Thank you, God, for sky and clouds.
Thank you, God, for sun and showers.
Thank you for our home, the earth—
For fruit and grain and flowers.

*This poem shows how some people say
thank you for all the good things in life.
How would you say thank you?
Think about it.*

DECEMBER

Basic Science Concepts:
Solid and Liquid
Sink and Float
Magnets, Electricity, Gravity
Sun and Shadows
Christmas around the World
Hanukkah

December!*

December, December,
Last month of the year—
December, December,
At last you are here!

I can remember
How last December
Was icy but bursting
With holiday cheer.

December, December,
We've waited so long
For your snowy splendor,
Your caroling song,

For garlands and ribbons
That wrap up the year—
December, December,
We're so glad you're here!

*May be sung to the tune of ''Sweet Betsy from Pike''

Solid, Liquid, Gas

Solids we bump into.
Liquids we jump into.
Solids can crash.
Liquids will splash.

Solids we can grab
and grip.
Not liquids—
they drip.

But air is a gas—
Not solid like brass
or liquid like juice.
Air is all loose!

Pouring*

Rice and beans
   Are fun to pour,
For when they spill
   Upon the floor,
You pick them up
   The way you oughta—
You can't do that
   With water!

What do you do when you spill water?
You can wipe it up, but you can't pick it up,
can you? How about juice? How about raisins?

*May be sung to the tune of "Oats, Peas, Beans"
(see also teacher's note 13).

Sink or Float*

Why does a lump of clay
In a pan full of water
   sink?
But the same lump of clay—
If shaped like a boat—
   will float!
It's strange. . . don't you think?

*See teacher's note 14.

Magnet

It grabs at things
Like pins and clips,
And pulls them by
Its fingertips.

It doesn't want
To let things go.
But how it holds them
I don't know!

What kinds of things can a magnet grab?
Can a magnet grab a piece of paper?

Electricity

If everything has
Electricity —
The air and the clouds
And even me —

Wouldn't you think
That I would glow,
And glimmer and shimmer
Wherever I go?

If I could switch myself
On — like a light —
I could see myself
In my room at night.

Why don't I light up
Like a Christmas tree
If all that stuff
Is inside of me?

Gravity. . .That's Why*

When you jump up,
Do you jump to the sky?
      NO!

When you jump up,
Do you fly-away-fly?
      NO!

Can you jump up
Right over the town?
      NO!

When you jump up,
Do you have to come down?
      YES!
Why?
      GRAVITY. . . HAVITY. . . GRAVITY!
      That's why.

*See teacher's note 15.

Making Shadows

The sun shines *on* and all *around,*
   But since it can't shine *through* me,
There's a shadow on the ground.
   Oh, it does nothing *to* me—
It's just the place where there's no light,
   A little darkness just like night.
I make it happen—so can you—
   Because the sun will not shine through.
That's something that it cannot do.

Can a lamp shine through you?
Or a flashlight? Why not?

Star

A star is something you can't touch.
A star is something far away.
Most stars are only seen at night,
But the sun's a star. . . we see by day!

Many Kinds of Christmas*

All over Norway on Christmas Eve
The bells of the churches sway
At four o'clock in the afternoon
To ring in Christmas Day.

In France the children set their shoes
On doorsteps, to be filled
With presents from *Le Petit Noël*,†
The beloved Christ Child.

In Italy there's a fairy queen
Who slides down chimneys because
She is *La Befana*, ‡
The lady Santa Claus!

On Christmas Day in Finland
There's ham and fish to eat.
But in Germany on Christmas Day,
Roast goose is the treat.

In Mexico at Christmas time
The merry choirs sing—
Where red and yellow flowers bloom—
December here is *spring*.

Christmas Day is joyful
In Oslo, Paris, Rome—
But my favorite kind of Christmas
Is the kind we have at home!

*See teacher's note 16
†/le pe • tee'/no • ell/
‡/lah bay • fah' nah/

Just a Fire

It's funny how a fire
In the fireplace
Can light up every
Friendly face
And warm us together
In the fiercest weather—
Just a fire
In the fireplace.

Toys, Toys!*

I want more.
Give me plenty.
Not just one or two—
But twenty.

Don't give *any*
To the others,
Not my sisters
Or my brothers.

Give them all
To me alone—
No matter how
They moan and groan.

The only things
That I might share
Are bits of sky
And sniffs of air.

And if they cry—
Well, I won't care.
So there! So there! So there!

What kind of child is this?
A sharing or a selfish child?
Are you selfish. . . or sharing?
*See teacher's note 17.

Christmas Is Coming*

Presents to make!
Songs to sing!
Cookies to bake!
Bells to ring!

Christmas is coming—
Let's light up the tree.
Santa Claus! Santa Claus!
Don't forget *me!*

*May be sung to the tune of "Hot Cross Buns"

Santa's Workshop*

This is the workshop
    Santa's elves
Built for you
    All by themselves—
With a *bang bang bang*
    And a *tap tap tap!*
To teach you how
    To fold and wrap!

*Christmas is not just a time to receive presents.
It's a time for giving, too.*

*See teacher's note 18.

In the Manger

The baby in the manger—
Did he cry?
Did his mother Mary sing to him
A lullaby?

The baby in the manger—
Did he know then
That he was being worshiped
By three Wise Men?

The baby in the manger—
Was he like no other child?
And was his mother like no other
When she smiled?

Hanukkah*

Feast of Lights

Eight days and nine candles,
Each lit one by one—
We say our blessings, eat our latkes,†
Then—what fun!

The dreidel‡ game—the little top
Spins and spins and spins.
The letter gimel§ faces up
And I'm the one who wins.

Our beautiful menorah
Stays all aglow with light.
Eight days—and gifts for us
Every single night!

*See teacher's note 19.
†/laht' kez/
‡/drayd' l/
§/gim' el/

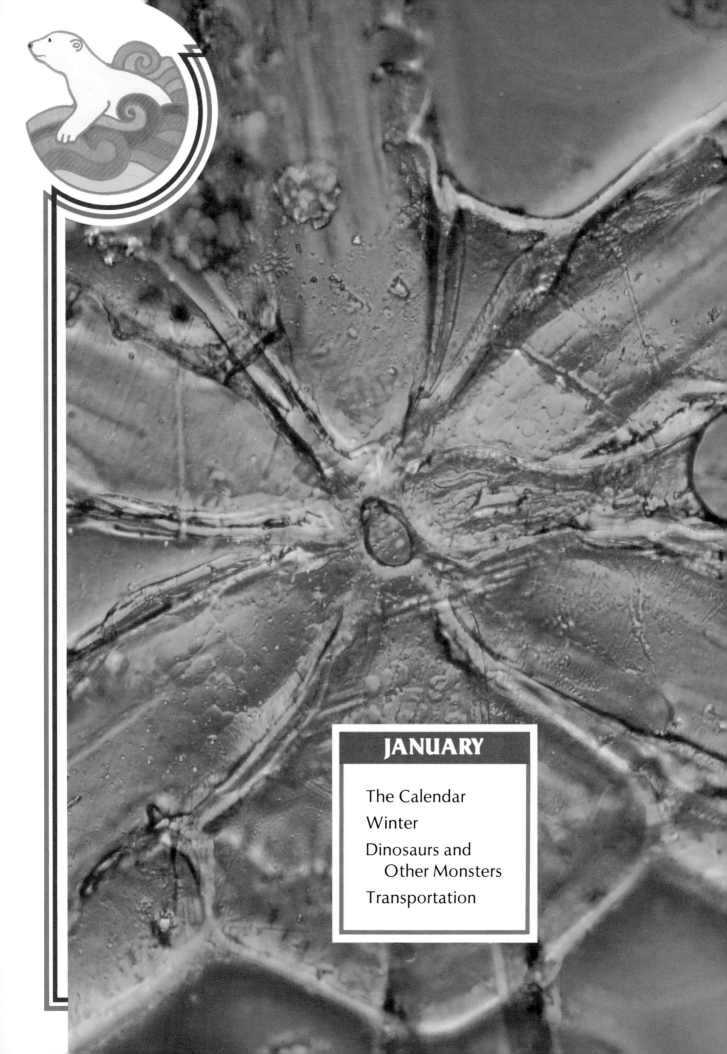

JANUARY

Old Year, New

January—one.
February—two.
March—three.
How do you do!

April—four.
May—five.
June—six.
Sakes alive!

July—seven.
August—eight.
September—nine.
Don't be late!

October—ten.
November—eleven.
December—twelve.
Now they're given—

Let's not wait.
It's time for us
To celebrate.
HAPPY NEW YEAR!

Frosting

On top of the cake—
    Frosting.
On top of my head—
    A hat.
On top of the house—
    A roof, of course.
But what's on top of that?

On top of the ground—
    Mountains.
On top of the mountains—
    Sky.
And up in the sky—
    Gobs of frosting,
The kind that goes drifting by.

What kind of "frosting" do we see in the sky?
Do you think a cloud would be good on a cake?
What would a cloud taste like?

The Wily Wind*

The wind has got inside the tree.
Its branches wave and sway.
The wind can't get inside of *me*—
I'm not made that way!

What does wily *mean?*
How are you different from a tree?
*May be sung to the tune of
"Row, Row, Row Your Boat"

Wintry Weather*

When it's windy, wet, or white,
You want and wish with all your might
To wake up from the winter storm
And find the sidewalk summer-warm.

But stubbornly it stays the way
You wanted it one summer day!
Want and wish with all your might—
Still it's windy, wet, or white.

When does everything get wet?
When does everything get white?
When it's summer, do you wish it were winter?
Now that it's winter, do you wish it were summer?
*See teacher's note 20.

Walking in the Snow

I step and sink
And step and sink.
There's nowhere I can get!
Even in my snow clothes
I'm cold clear through
And wet!

I step and sink
And step and sink.
There's snow inside my boots!
I might as well
Pretend that I'm
A tree with feet for roots.

Fog

It's a cold blanket
To be wrapped up in—
Only a cloud,
Wet and thin,
That never seems
To end or begin. . .

Have you ever walked in the fog?
You wouldn't want to sleep under a blanket
of fog, would you? Brrrr!

Catching Cold Doesn't Start with "K" (But Sneezing Does)

K-K-K-Kerchoo! K-K-K-Kerchoo!
I should have worn a kerchief on my head.
K-K-K-Kerchoo! K-K-K-Kerchoo!
Now I have to K-K-K in bed.

Stay Out of Puddles!

Teach your feet
To tell your shoes
Never to forget
To stay away from puddles that
Are plentiful
And wet!

*When is it all right to step
in puddles and when is it not?
Stomping through puddles and splashing
other people is bad puddle manners.*

It's Raining!*

The sky turned gray
And hid the blue.
The grass got wet,
The sidewalk, too.

Let's stay inside
And sip the sound
Of raindrops touching
Roof and ground.

***May be sung to the tune of
"It's Raining, It's Pouring"**

Sharing the Storm

Lightning cracks the heavy sky
and sends the thunder drumming.
The rains come down, and Mom and I
get all curled up, as nice as pie,
in the easy chair.
And there—
where it's so snug and warm—
we share the wonder
of the storm.

Which comes first? The lightning
or the thunder? Why?
Did you ever share a storm?
Who did you share it with?

Sleeping Bag

I slip inside the smooth, wide mouth—
Scooch down to where it's warm.
Inside my creature's tummy now,
I'll hibernate through the storm.

Doors can rattle, windows shake—
I'm safe inside my beast.
Let him think he's swallowed me—
We'll both enjoy the feast!

What does it mean to hibernate?
Can you think of some
animals that hibernate?
If your sleeping bag were an animal,
what kind would it be?

The Dinosaur That Knocked

A dinosaur bigger than your house or mine
Came to our street at a quarter past nine.
His eyes, way up high, were as distant as stars.
But with big clumsy feet, he stepped. . .*CRUNCH*. . .on our cars.

He knocked on our door and our whole house shook.
My mother was wearing a horrified look.
I told her, "Don't worry. I'll handle this guy."
And I hollered at him till I thought he would cry.

I said, "What do you think you're doing out there?
You crunch people's cars and you don't even care.
What do you want? This is no place to play."
And he answered me softly, "I've lost my way. . .

"I need a few barrels of something to eat—
And I'd like to sit down and rest my feet."
There wasn't a chair anywhere he could sit in.
On the whole darned street—not a house he could *fit* in!

What could I do with a creature like this?
I sure couldn't give him a hug and a kiss!
I thought and I thought till it hurt my head,
And finally. . .this is what I said:

"You've got the wrong time, the wrong place, the wrong year.
Dinosaurs don't belong *now* or *here*."
And with that he proceeded to disappear.

After he left us, we put up a sign.
It said DINOSAURS, GO SOMEWHERE ELSE TO DINE!
And he never came back, which is perfectly fine.

What Monsters Eat

Monsters eat a special dish—
It's made of bricks and bones.
Add a hunk of smelly fish,
And don't forget some stones.

Monsters like a little bit
Of pepper, lots of salt,
And sugar by the barrelful.
It's really not their fault—

They can't help being monsters.
(You can't help being *you*.)
I hope you never have to eat
A bowl of monster stew!

Ways to Go!*

The wonderful thing about a bus
    (Yes, it's true.)
Is that it can hold so many of us,
    (Yes, it's true.)
And we can sit wherever we like—
You can't do that upon a bike. . .
    (Golly, Polly, yes it's true!)

The wonderful thing about a plane
    (Yes, it's true.)
Is that it can fly up over the rain—
    (Yes, it's true.)
For it can soar above the clouds,
Over the buildings, over the crowds. . .
    (Golly, Polly, yes it's true!)

The wonderful thing about a ship
    (Yes, it's true.)
Is that we can slowly take a trip,
    (Yes, it's true.)
And we can sail from shore to shore
Of places we've never seen before. . .
    (Golly, Polly, yes it's true!)

The wonderful thing about a car
    (Yes, it's true.)
Is that it can go so very far
    (Yes, it's true.)
And never ever leave the ground
And pass through every street and town. . .
    (Golly, Polly, yes it's true!)

*May be sung to the tune of
"Hinky Dinky Parlez-Vous"

All Aboard*

We lined up chairs in the hallway
And called it a railroad car.
Annie and I were passengers—
We were going to go so far!

Elizabeth served us sandwiches
With a pickle chip or two.
David came and sat behind us.
Then the whistle blew—

And everybody waited
For the train to roll away
That gray and rainy afternoon
On a nothing-to-do day.

We brought our books and read them,
And sat so very still
While the wheels went round inside our heads
Over each imagined hill.

*See teacher's note 21.

Zinger the Swinger

Zinger the swinger
Is full of pizzazz.
He loves cars
And he loves jazz.

He's full of zest
And full of zeal.
He zips around
In his automobile.

From zone to zone
And finger to finger,
Zig zag zig
Goes zippy Zinger.

Place your right forefinger at the top of the left thumb and move it down, finger by finger, to the top of the little finger and back again, with each stanza.

FEBRUARY

Groundhog Day

Groundhog crawled out
Of her burrow today.
She saw her own shadow
And got scared away.

"Six more weeks of winter!"
The farmers declared.
They should have hid her shadow
So she wouldn't get scared!

Groundhog Day is February 2.
What is a groundhog?
Can you hide a shadow?

Abraham Lincoln

He was a tall man
With a tall hat.
He even looked tall
When he sat.

He was a good man
And an honest one.
He was glad to go
To Washington—

Glad he was
The one we sent
To be our sixteenth
President.

George Washington

George Washington
Was a gentleman
And a soldier brave and fine.
The people made him president
In 1789.

George Washington
Was number one.
He was the first to be
President of a United States
That was young and bold and free.

Post Office*

Step inside!
Stamps for sale!
Packages, post cards,
Letters to mail!

Come to us
For your money's worth.
Deliveries made
All over the earth!

*See teacher's note 22.

Hearts*

Scissors, cut straight.
Oh scissors, be neat.
Scissors, make circles
And hearts so sweet.

Make them for someone
I love so well
For Valentine's Day—
But please, don't tell!

*May be sung to the tune of "Little Boy Blue"

Friends

Friends smile at you.
They like your face.
They want to be with you
Any old place.

Friends have fun with you.
Friends share.
They're glad when you're happy—
When you're sad, they care.

If you're a friend,
Then you care, too.
That's why your friends
Are glad you're you.

Nice and New

New things are nice,
Like lunch pails and shoes.
But not every new thing
Is to wear or to use.

A new person came
To our class yesterday.
She moved to our town
From a place far away.

We asked if she'd play with us—
Hopscotch or ball.
And now she is going to be
Friends with us all!

Do you think you can have too many friends?
Wouldn't it be nice to be friends with everybody?

Boy, Was I Mad!

I got so mad this morning,
I threw our stove in the air.
It didn't come down till lunchtime.
But I didn't care.

I got so mad this morning,
I blew the fireplace down.
I blew it right on out the door
And clear across town.

I got so mad this morning,
I made my mother cry.
She cried so many tears, I said,
"Go bake a teardrop pie!"

I got so mad this morning,
I made the whole earth shake.
It shook until the mountains fell,
And *that* was a mistake.

What do you do when you get mad?
Do you do things you shouldn't?

Feelings

My feelings are funny —
And full of surprise.
Inside my tummy
They're butterflies.

They can turn me red
In my cheeks and ears,
Or ooze from my eyes
In salty tears.

They can make my arms
Go all goose-bumpy.
In my feet
They're happy-jumpy!

Have you ever had butterflies or goose bumps?
Are you ever so happy that you feel like jumping
up and down?

Can't*

You can't be a cowboy
If you don't have a cow.
You can't be a puppy
If you can't say, "Bow-wow."

You can't tell, "It hurts!"
If you can't yell, "Ow!"
And you shouldn't say, "Can't"
When you just. . .don't know how!

When you think you can't do something, sometimes it's because you don't know how. Sometimes it's because you haven't practiced enough.
*See teacher's note 23.

Being the Best You Can Be

You have to practice.
The fact is, you have to.
You have to practice, whatever you do.
If it's sewing a seam or dreaming a dream,
You have to practice to make it come true.

You have to practice, whatever your goal is,
If it's dancing or flying a kite.
Whatever appears to be wrong, believe me,
Practice can set it right.

What is practice but trying—
And knowing you're growing—
And seeing you're being
The best you can be!

If you want to add or subtract
Or put on a magical act,
You have to practice—
And that is a fact.

Happy

I'm so happy
I could leap to the moon!
I'm so happy
I could dance with a baboon!

There's such gladness inside me,
My mouth won't turn down—
It just keeps on smiling—
It forgot how to frown.

I feel so good—
I don't know what I'll do.
My goodness! My smile
Is spreading to you!

What makes you feel happy? What makes you smile?
What happens when you frown? Does your frown spread
to other people?

Where Is Love?

Love is where you find it.
You only have to look.
It's in the birds and butterflies
And down along the brook.

Love is on the mountain.
Love is in the sky.
Love is in the earth below
And in the clouds up high.

God has placed love everywhere—
Though it's not on maps or charts.
Best of all, He sent His love
To fill our minds and hearts.

Love Is

Love is bright
When skies are gray.
Love can warm
The coldest day.

Love is right
When things go wrong.
In noisy places,
Love is song.

Love's a message—
Bright eyes shine
To say, "Please be
My valentine!"

Main Street*

There's a busy little shop
With trumpets and guitars,
And a shop full of tires
For trucks and cars.

There's a hardware store
Where people buy nails
And hammers and saws
And ladders and pails.

There's a jewelry store
With watches and rings
And a hobby shop
With all sorts of things.

But my favorite place
Has goldfish and guppies
And a monkey in the window
And some kittens and puppies!

*See teacher's note 24.

Jolly Job Hunters*

John got a job as a jockey.
Joe got a job in a jail.
Joyce got a job in a jewelry store,
With jasper and jade for sale.

Jack got a job as a juggler.
Jules got a job driving jeep.
Jim got a job on a jury,
But the judge kept falling asleep.

Jud got a job in a junkyard,
Piling up broken-down cars.
But Jill got the jolliest job of all,
Tasting jellies and jams in jars!

*See teacher's note 25.

MARCH

Spring
Outdoors
Little Creatures
St. Patrick's Day
Purim

Silly Soup*

Silly soup is made with snow,
  Made with snow,
  Made with snow.
Silly soup is made with snow
And served to snails in spring—

With salad leaves to help them grow,
  Help them grow,
  Help them grow—
With salad leaves to help them grow
And sandwiches that sing!

*May be sung to the tune of "London Bridge"

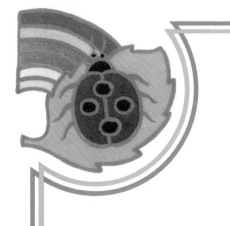

Swinging*

I love to swing,	*(Swing both arms)*
Back and forth,	
Back and forth.	
I love to swing	*(Swing both arms and*
In the yard,	*right leg)*
Not too high,	*(Left leg)*
Not too hard.	
I love to swing	*(Right leg)*
And swing	
And swing.	
It's my very	*(Left leg)*
Favorite thing!	
	(Jump up and clap your hands)

*See teacher's note 26.

See-Saw

See-saw up!	*(Start from squatting*
	position—stand)
See-saw down!	*(Squat)*
See-saw, we saw	*(Stand)*
A silly old clown.	*(Squat)*
See-saw high!	*(Repeat actions)*
See-saw low!	
He was wearing	
A big red bow.	
See-saw up!	*(Repeat)*
See-saw down!	
See-saw, we saw	
A silly old clown.	
See-saw high!	*(Repeat)*
See-saw low!	
See-saw, a bumblebee	
Bit his toe!	
Oh!	*(Hop around holding your*
	foot)

Kite

Little by little
We let out the string.
Little by little
Our kite takes wing.

Up. . .up. . .up. . .
Into a cloud.
"Come on, kite!"
I shout out loud.

There it goes!
Way up high!
Swooping and sweeping
The afternoon sky.

Down. . .down. . .
Without a sound.
Down it comes
To touch the ground.

*Pretend you are a kite
on the end of a string.
What kind of kite are you?
What does it feel like
to be flying in the wind?*

Ladybug

Ladybug wears
An orange cape.
It opens up
And changes shape—

Now two wings lift her
Into the air.
I wish I had
Such a cape to wear!

*Have you ever had a ladybug
rest on your hand?
Was her cape orange?*

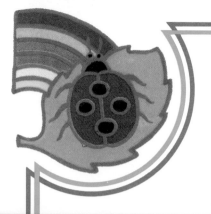

Bees

Bees that buzz
Around my nose —   (Touch nose)
I tell you, I'm not
Fond of those.

Bees that buzz
At my elbows and knees —   (Touch elbows,
No sir, I'm not   knees)
Fond of these.

But bees that buzz
Near flower and stem,
Making honey —
I like them.
   Mmmmm!   (Lick lips)

Is honey sweet or sour?
Is a lemon sweet or sour?
How about lemonade?

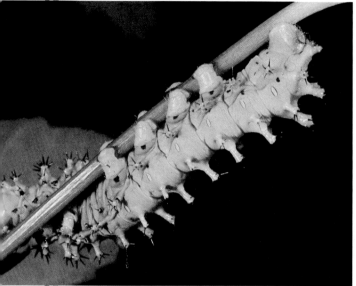

Caterpillar

Caterpillar hurries
To eat all he can eat.
He munches and he chews his way
Along the leafy street.

Caterpillar scurries
Because — very soon —
He is going to find himself
Wrapped in a cocoon.

Inside his silky wrapping,
Caterpillar sleeps.
He no longer goes for walks,
No longer crawls or creeps.

Nobody feeds him,
Not a crumb of bread or pie.
But Caterpillar doesn't care —
Now he's Butterfly!

Spider

My little friend the spider
Can speed across the wall.

*(Fingers of right hand crawl in
left palm and run up arm to shoulder)*

He can creep across the ceiling
Without any help at all.

*(Go up and over head
and on all stop on
shoulder)*

My little friend the spider—
How can he be complete?
How can he crawl around so fast
Without any hands or feet?

*(Repeat, starting with fingers of
left hand in right palm)*

*Did you ever see a spider with hands or feet?
How many legs does a spider have?*

Opposites

Spider crawls on tippy-fingers.
Spider creeps on tippy-toes.

*(Right fingers crawl from
left palm to shoulder)*

He doesn't want a soul to hear him
When he's going where he goes.

*(Right fingers stay on left
shoulder; left fore-
finger to lips; say "Shhh"
and shake your head no.)*

But Fly announces when he's near

*(Right thumb and forefinger
form a circle.)*

By buzz buzz buzzing in my ear.

(Circle the right ear.)

You'd think that he would rather not

*(Left thumb and forefinger
form a circle.)*

Make known that he is there
            to swat!

*(Circle the left ear.)
(Slap right thigh!)*

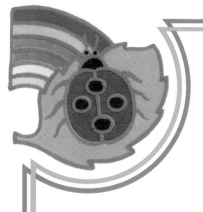

If I Were a Snail

If I were as soft
As a snail is. . .well,
You can be sure
I'd live in a shell.

You'd know where I went
By my silvery track.
But you might not know
If I'd ever come back.

If I were a snail
And was feeling shy,
I'd be too embarrassed
To say good-bye.

And seeing as how
I was so very slow,
I might *not* get around
To saying hello.

*Have you ever noticed the silver trails
that snails leave behind them?*

Big Fat Toad

I've watched him eating
Beetles and bugs
And fireflies and earthworms
And slippery slugs.

No wonder he's gotten
So big and fat!
If I ate like him,
Would I look like that?

*What do toads eat?
Listen again. . .*

Sparrow

She scurries along
With eyes like beads,
Down the path
And through the weeds.

An early supper
Is on her mind.
What do you suppose
She'll find?

I'll toss her crumbs
And see if she
Wants to come
Make friends with me.

If so, I'll give her
All my bread
And stroke her tiny
Sparrow head.

If not—if she
Prefers the grass,
I guess I'll have to
Let her pass.

Earthworm

What does he see
under the ground?
Squirming and worming
himself around. . .

Wriggling and wiggling
along his way,
How can he tell
if it's night or day?

If I had to do
all that squirming
and squiggling,
I'd burst out giggling!

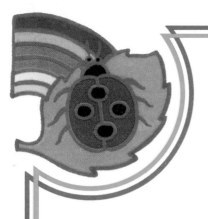

Rainbow*

A rainbow leaped
Out of the air
And flung itself
From here to there—

It made a bridge
Across the sky.
But no one climbed it—
I wonder why.

Why can't you climb a rainbow bridge?
***May be sung to the tune of
"A Tisket, A Tasket"**

A Purim Poem*

We have costumes and dancing—
The girls and boys
Twirl their gragers†
To make lots of noise.

We have presents to give—
Little cakes and things.
Oh, what happiness
Purim brings!

*See teacher's note 27.
†/grog' erz/

St. Patrick's Day

March seventeen—
Don't be seen
Unless you're wearing
A touch of green.

A skirt, a shirt,
A button, a sock—
A splash of green
From the old shamrock.

If you don't wear green—
So the Irish say—
You deserve a pinch
For St. Patrick's Day!

Imp O'Light

I met an imp
Called Imp O'Light.
He never smiled,
But he would fight!

He interrupted
When people spoke.
Whatever he played with,
He always broke.

If someone begged him,
"Be quiet—please,"
He stuck out his tongue
And wiggled his knees.

Some kids decided
It wouldn't do
To let him bother
Good people like you.

They caught him when
He was yelling at lunch.
They said, "You behave!"
But he started to punch.

"Behave!" cried the imp.
"I'll never behave!"
So they dragged him off
To a faraway cave.

The kids said, "This
Is where you'll stay
If you can't be good."
Then they marched away.

Now deep in the cave
Where it's dark and cold,
All by himself
Imp O'Light grows old.

The kids have to keep him
Out of sight,
That rude little imp
Called Imp O'Light.

*What if there were a cave inside of
you. . .and a rude little imp lived in there?
Would you want to let him out?*

APRIL

April Fool's Day
Easter
Passover
Flowers
Pets

April First

The Queen of England's coming!
And our President, too!
And a lady who's from London
And a man who's from Peru!

They're coming to our class today—
They want to see our school.
Oh my goodness! Oh my goodness!
April Fool!

*April Fools' Day is also called
All Fools' Day. It's a day to play
jokes on people, but always in fun—
never to hurt anyone.*

Different Hats

Each time you wear
A different hat,
Whatever it is,
You are that!

Put one on
And you will see.
Whatever it is,
You must be.

Hat Shop*

Hats! Hats! A hundred hats!
Yellow, pink, and blue.
Silly, pretty, useful hats. . .
Flowery, floppy too.

Hats! Hats! A hundred hats!
Some are old, some new.
Mirror, mirror on the wall
Knows just the one for you.

*See teacher's note 28.

Easter Eggs

Dip
one
in
dye. . .
Purple. . .red.
Give it a face.
Put hair on its head.
Dip
one
in
dye. . .
Yellow. . .blue.
If it turns green,
what will we do?
Dip
strips
of
color. . .
This one is funny.
I think I'll save it
for the Easter Bunny.
Don't you suppose
he likes Easter eggs too?
I've never asked him.
Have you?

It's Passover*

Everything shines like a room full of lights
For this night is different from all other nights.

We've scrubbed every corner—twice, at least.
It's seder!† Tonight is our special feast!

There'll be lots of food—and matzo‡ bread,
And questions to ask after blessings are said—

And prayers and songs and a game to play.
And everything's done in a special way—

A wonderfully special way because
It's Passover.

*See teacher's note 29.
†/sayd'er/
‡/maht'zuh/

Gabriel's Garden*

Gabriel grew a garden.
Golly, it was good.
It grew and grew and grew and grew,
The way a garden should.

Gabriel's Grandpa asked him,
"How do you do it, lad?
The grass keeps getting greener.
The gladiolas are so glad!

"Do you wear a magic glove, my boy?
How does your garden grow?"
"Water, sunshine, love," said Gabe.
"And it helps to have a hoe."

What is a hoe? What is it for?
*See teacher's note 30.

How Flowers Grow

Ask the elves
How flowers grow.
Ask the elves—
They should know.

They live inside
The blossoms bright,
And take their baths
In flower light.

They know what makes
A flower bloom,
And what gives blossoms
Sweet perfume.

I know they know,
For I myself
Discussed the matter
With an elf.

He told me
Everything he knew.
Just ask an elf
And he'll tell you.

Kitty

Kitty has a clever way
Of keeping to herself all day.
But evenings when I'm in my chair,
She curls up close and cuddles there.
She lets me know she'd disapprove
If I should leave. . .
Or even move!

Tiny Turtle

My turtle crawls
Just like a baby.
Does he know he's slow?
Maybe.

Though he's not cuddly,
I still love him.
Does he know I'm here
Above him?

Can he see all
My shape and size
With his tiny
Turtle eyes?

He must think
I'm big and smart.
Bless his little
Turtle heart!

The Tap-Dancing Cat

Tap Tap Patty,   *(Clap hands and stamp*
The tap-dancing cat,   *right foot, two times on*
Wore bows on her tail   *each line; stress same*
And flags in her hat.   *rhythm throughout)*

She tapped on two feet.   *(Repeat with left foot)*
She tapped on four.
She tapped all over
The kitchen floor.

Tap tap Patty   *(Repeat with right foot)*
Caught a rat.
Had to let him go—
And that was that!

Repeat entire poem,
starting with left foot.

Pup

Puppy runs to me. . .
   Lippity lop.
He has fun with me. . .
   Flippity flop.
And he gives a soft *grrr*
As I ruffle his fur
From his tail to his
   Tippity top!

Diddly Duck

Diddly Duck's Dad
Said, "Diddly, don't."
Diddly said,
"Oh Dad, I won't!"

But Diddly did it—
I wouldn't kid.
Diddly did it—
He really did.

What did he do
That he shouldn't have done?
Diddly didn't
Hurt anyone.

He followed a girl
And became her pet.
But Diddly's Dad
Doesn't know it yet. . .

*Did you know that ducks will follow
people and become their pets?*

Hamster*

Wiggle wiggle
Goes his nose.
Wiggle wiggle. . .
Do you suppose

He's sniffing something
I can't smell?
Whatever it is,
He won't tell.

Hurry scurry
All around. . .
What do you
Suppose he's found?

He stops, sits up,
And squeals as if
He thinks that *I*
Should also sniff!

*See teacher's note 31.

Wendell's Goat

Wendell's goat was brown as a sack
With one black stripe right down his back,
One black ear and four black feet.
He didn't smell too awful sweet.
But that was not the explanation
For Wendell's goat's big reputation.

Beneath the back porch Billy would sleep.
When visitors came, out he'd creep.
Then suddenly that goat would *leap*—
Onto the cow barn, onto the shack,
Onto anything you'd stack.
Onto the henhouse, and then he'd commence
To walk along the backyard fence!

Onto the visitors' shiny car roofs
Billy would go with his four sharp hoofs.
It made them mad from time to time,
But Billy goats are born to climb—
So Wendell said. He was willing to bet
No one had a more talented pet.

Wendell gave Billy a hug so warm—
He encouraged that goat to get up and perform.
And when the town held its circus-bazaar,
Wendell's goat was the natural star!

The Petting Zoo

Step inside.
Touch the goat.
Let him nibble
At your coat.

Give the lamb
A little hug.
He feels just like
A woolly rug!

Watch the chicken
Standing near —
She might peck you
On your ear.

Sit on the tortoise,
So big and still.
You'd hardly know
That he is real!

Hug the fuzzy
Wiggle-nosed rabbit.
Petting can get to be
Quite a nice habit.

The Perfect Pet*

Give me a pet that's purple
With a tiny touch of pink —
One that will swim in the water
And not necessarily sink.

His eyes should be round as buttons.
His tail — I want to see through.
Could he have a few spots on his belly?
And a stripe, at least one or two?

*I'm sure you don't mean a kitten,
Or the usual kind of puppy.
Perhaps you'd prefer a tropical fish.
That's it! Give me one guppy!*

*See teacher's note 32.

It's May*

Good morning, Mrs. Bird,
And how are you today?
Good morning, Mr. Butterfly.
Do you know it's May?

Good morning, Mr. Sun.
You must be the one
Who sent sweet April on her way
So merry May could come.

How did the sun send April away?

***May be sung to the tune of
"Sing a Song of Sixpence"**

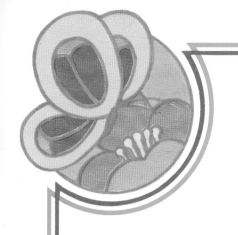

Mothers Are. . .

Mothers are music at night
And soft moonbeams.
Mothers are making things right
And sharing our dreams.

Mothers are tucking us in
And having our secrets to keep.
Mothers are who we love
Even while we sleep.

A Gift for Mother*

What shall I give to Mother,
Who gives so much to me?
A bright bouquet of flowers?
A young and growing tree?

A book, a bird, a bracelet,
Fancy paper and a pen. . .
I think I've found her just the thing.
I *think* I have, but then. . .

What shall I give, I wonder,
That can't be made or bought?
Something extra special,
Full of extra special thought—

I'll give her what she gives to me—
A smile, a helping way.
I'll give it not just once a year,
But every single day!

*May be sung to the tune of
"I Had a Little Nut Tree"
(play the first part of the song
three times for the first three stanzas).

Mom and I

She drives off to work
Bright and early—
Her clothes all neat,
Her hair all curly.

And I go to school
On the big school bus.
We work all day,
The two of us.

Then, in the evening,
Over our meal,
We share with each other
The way we feel.

Do you share your feelings with your Mom?
With someone else? It's important to
share our feelings with someone, isn't it?

The Picture Album

In our picture album
You can see
A teeny-tiny baby,
And the baby is me.

I'm wrapped in a blanket
And I'm so very small,
You'd never ever guess
That I could grow this tall.

You'd never ever guess
That I'd do the things I do,
Seeing what I looked like
When I was new.

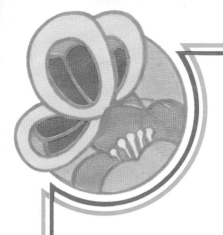

My Accident*

I stumbled on the sidewalk
And skinned my knee,
Trying to catch my brother
As he ran away from me.

My mother said, "Oh baby!"
(Although I'm really not).
My father said, "Come here, sweet.
Let's see what you've got."

So I cried and let them hug me
And bandage up the hurt,
And now, although it's only three,
I get to have dessert!

*See teacher's note 33.

The Toothpick Family*

The toothpick house is tiny.
It was built by the toothpick man.
He's got a very skinny wife—
They drive a toothpick van.

They're sort of poor but happy.
Their children are just slivers.
When it's cold on frosty nights,
The toothpick family shivers.

*See teacher's note 34.

Peas, Please

Anne, Anne
   hasn't a plan.
She hasn't a wish
   because her dish
   is full of peas.
Believe it or not,
   there is nothing like these
   to please Anne.
"Peas, peas," Anne would say
   at least a dozen times a day.
We thought that she couldn't pronounce her *L.*
   But "Peas!" she would holler,
   and "Peas!" she would yell.
In a bowl or a dish,
   in a pot or a pan,
   only peas would satisfy Anne.
With carrots, with butter, with salt, with bran,
   with *anything,* peas will please sweet Anne.
Anne, Anne
   (that's where we began)
She can't say *please,* but she can say *peas.*
   "PEAS, PEAS!"
She certainly can.

Do you have a little brother or sister? Can he or she say l's?
Can you? Say please. *Do you hear the* l *that comes after the* p?

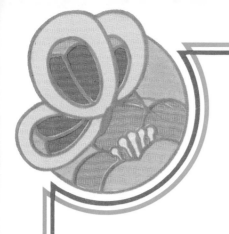

The Grocery Store

There's a grocery store
At the end of town.
You walk inside
And you never sit down.

They've got no chairs—
All they have is aisles—
Rows of stuff
For miles and miles.

You walk around
And fill your cart
With milk and fruit,
And you feel so smart.

But you can't leave the store
(This part is funny)
Till you stop at the counter
And give someone money.

General Store*

GENERAL STORE—
The place to buy beans
And flour and butter
And brand new jeans.

We have boots,
Both narrow and wide.
Please leave horses
And holsters outside.

*See teacher's note 35.

Shopping for Mom

A loaf of lettuce,
A head of bread,
A quart of eggs. . .
That's what she said.

A pound of juice
And a can of pie.
I can't find anything!
I wonder why. . .

A loaf of. . .? What should it be? Not lettuce.
A head of. . .?
A quart of. . .?
What about eggs?

Animal Families

Silky, squeaky
Baby pig,
Will you grow
To be as big
As your father the hog
And your mother the sow?
We wouldn't think so
To see you now.

Wibbly wobbly
Little calf,
You'll soon be frisky
And make us laugh.
Your mother the dam,
Your father the bull
Think that you are
Beautiful.

Woolly woolly
Baby lamb,
Your mother's a ewe,
Your father's a ram.
Do you know
Who I am?

I'm a child
Who's always had
A mother that's Mom
And a father that's Dad.

The Cows*

The cows in the pasture
Are peaceful as pies,
Flipping their tails
To shoo away flies.

There's no one to tell them
What they should do,
So they lazily graze,
Making more cuds to chew.

*See teacher's note 36.

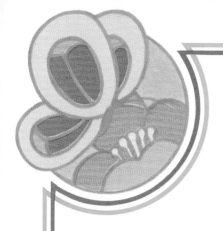

The Foal

The newborn foal
Blinks his bright eyes.
See his fuzzy tail?
He can barely rise.

He can hardly stand.
But in no time at all,
You'll see him bolting
From this stall

Into the open
To kick up his heels
And find out how
The pasture feels.

Chick

Chick
pecked
pecked
his way
out of
the shell.
Now
here he is
all wobbly
and wet.
Well,
give an hour or two
for his feathers to dry—
He'll be soft and fluffy
by
and by.

If You Want
to Be a Cowboy

If you want to be a cowboy,
I can tell you how, boy.
If you want to be a cowboy, just you listen now
    to me.
Buy yourself a saddle.
Go out and find some cattle,
And leave behind the noises of the townfolks'
    jamboree.*

Wear some boots with pointy toes 'n
Wear some tightly-fitting clothes 'n
Wear some leather chaps to keep the thorns
    from tearing at your pants.
Have a wide sombrero hat.
(You won't be needing a cravat†—
You'll be far away from church and school
    and dance.)

Wear some spiny silver spurs.
Have a handy knife for chores.
Strap your saddle on securely and be sure
    to carry rope.
Get used to beans and bacon.
Get used to muscles achin'.
Get used to no hot water and very little soap.

So you want to be a cowboy.
Well, that's what you are now, boy.
You've got everything to start you on your
    course.
You've got all that it takes
To handle varmints, critters, snakes.
But oops! It looks like we forgot one thing—
    a horse!

*A jamboree is a party.
†A cravat is a necktie.

JUNE

Fathers

Summer
    Vacation
Travel

Zoo Animals

It's June

June! June!
Jump up! It's June!
School is going to be
Over soon.

We'll go on vacation
Across the nation
And lie in the sun
All afternoon—
Because it's June.
Jump up! It's June!

Dad

Dads come in different sizes—
Some are short, and some are tall.
Some play chess and checkers,
And some play basketball.

Some Dads do the cooking,
And some Dads mow the lawn.
Some are home almost all the time,
And some are sometimes gone.

Our Dad has to travel—
We don't see him every day.
But when he's home from where he's been,
The whole house shouts, "Hooray!"

The Motor Home*

We pile into Grandpa's motor home
And *bumpity bump* along.
We sit at the table as we ride,
Singing our favorite song.

We go to the beach
Or sometimes the park,
And we get to play
Till it's almost dark.

In the tiny kitchen
We fix our meals,
While Grandpa snoozes
In his house on wheels.

When it's time to leave,
We moan and groan,
Then *bumpity bump*
Our way back home.

*See teacher's note 37.

At the Lake*

One step, two step—
Through the sand.
Three step, four step—
Isn't it grand?

To the water—
Five step—dash!
Here I come!
Six, seven, *splash*!

*See teacher's note 38.

Alphabet Soup

I slurped an S. I bit a B.
I spilled an XYZ on me.
I chewed C-H. I drank D-R.
And then I spelled myself a CAR.

The Car Wash

Enter the box.
First the water sprays down.
Then the whirling black brush
Rolls slowly over us,
Over our tops and down our backs.
Shh! Shh! Whirr! Whirr!
Over our heads and down our backs.

The big round cleaners
Spin at our sides—
To the left, to the right—
Rubbing and scrubbing from front to back.

The long red strips
Sway before us
Like octopus arms.
Swish! Swish!
Over the windshield,
Wiping our tops and wiping our backs.

The water runs down, like after a rain,
And then it runs up
In quick little lines
As the wheels of the dryer,
The hot air dryer,
Go over our heads and down our backs.
Shh! Shh! Out of the box.
We're clean!

Takeoff*

Slow
slow
inching slow
creeping slow
turning slow

Now here we go!
faster
faster
past the hangers
over the trees.

The cars are like toys.
The trucks and vans
on the freeway below
grow smaller and smaller
the higher we go.

The yards and lawns
are tiny patches.
The trees are like matches.
We're up so high!
Higher we fly—
over mountains of clouds
all rolling and white.
But the sun shines bright
on our big jet plane,
our beautiful big jet plane.

*See teacher's note 40.

What Did I Take
on My Vacation?*

I took my vacuum cleaner.
I took my gorilla.
I took my vinegar.
I took my vanilla.

I took a violin.
I took a diaper.
I took a vampire.
I took a viper.

I took some vegetables.
I took a pan.
Then I drove to Venice
In a very nice van.

*See teacher's note 39.

What Do They Do?

All over Europe
What do boys do
When they're tired?
They sleep, just like you do.

In South America
What do girls do
When they're having fun?
They laugh, just like you do.

Down in Australia
What do kids do
When it's dinnertime?
They eat. Wouldn't you?

In the faraway Orient
What do friends do
When they meet?
They smile, like me and you.
They do what *we* do.

By Any Name, I'm Still the Same!*

In Germany I'm Johann.
I'm Jean when I'm in France.
The Russians call me Ivan
Without a second glance.

Italians say, "Giovanni!"
In Mexico it's "Juan!"
But that's okay. Since you're my friend,
You can call me *John*.

*What about your name? Do you think your name
would be different in another country?*

*See teacher's note 41.

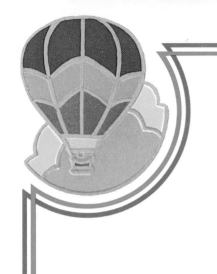

My Beautiful Balloon

I'm standing in a basket
Pretending a balloon,
A big one, is above my head.
Hang on! We're leaving soon!

Now I feel it rising,
High above the trees.
I'm floating like a butterfly
On an afternoon breeze.

Flying over cities,
Drifting over farms—
Everything looks little
As I start to wave my arms.

I see the tiny people
Shouting from below—
They wish that they could be with me
And go where I will go.

*Would flying with a big balloon be different
from flying in an airplane? How?*

Zoo*

One striped tiger,
Two fat hippos,
Three thick rhinoceroses,
Four tall giraffes,
Five spotted leopards,
Six lazy lions,
Seven gorillas on the grass—
All ignore us as we pass.

*See teacher's note 42.

Mama's Little Baby*

Mama's little baby has black stripes, white stripes,
Mama's little baby has black and white stripes.
 What is Mama's little baby?

Mama's little baby has a long, long, long, long,
Mama's little baby has a long, long, neck.
 What is Mama's little baby?

Mama's little baby has great big floppy ears,
Mama's little baby has great big ears,
 What is Mama's little baby?

Mama's little baby is in her pouch now,
Mama's little baby is in her pouch.
 What is Mama's little baby?

*May be sung to the tune of "Shortnin' Bread"
(see also teacher's note 43).

Joey

Joey is a baby 'roo.
He has nothing else to do
But stay inside his mother's purse.
Can you imagine anything worse?

Yet Joe's as happy in that pocket
As you and I'd be in a rocket
Soaring off to outer space.
He prefers his inner place.
It fits him like a glove or shoe.
It's made for Baby Kangaroo.

Monkey Business*

The monkey swings from branch to branch
And never ever misses.
He jumps at every single chance.
What fun all this is!

*May be sung to the tune of ''Pop Goes the Weasel''
(see also teacher's note 44).

The Elephant Walk*

The elephant lumbers
on stumpy legs,
planting his big round
feet as he goes,
with a swinging trunk
and squinting eyes
and skin like a map
of the places he knows.

*Have you ever looked at an elephant's skin?
It has lines criss-crossing all over it
like lines on a map.
Imagine you're an elephant with thick legs
and big round feet. Let your arm be your
trunk. Squint your eyes. Do the elephant walk.*
*See teacher's note 45.

JULY

Fireworks*

BOOM! go the fireworks.
BOOM! in the night.
BOOM! they burst
Into golden light.

BOOM! go the fireworks.
BOOM! after dark.
BOOM! Red stars
All scatter and spark.

BOOM! go the fireworks
Over the town.
BOOM! Green lights
Come dripping down.

BOOM! go the fireworks
Up in the sky.
BOOM! BOOM!
It's the Fourth of July!

*See teacher's note 46.

On the Fourth

On the fourth of July, we fly our flag
And pack our lunches in a bag.
We picnic over at the park,
And stick around until it's dark.
We watch the fireworks display—
HAPPY BIRTHDAY, U.S.A.
What a special, sparkly day!

Yankee Doodle Dandy*

Yankee Doodle, who are you?
A soldier in the army.
What's a dandy? He's a fellow
All dressed up to charm thee.

Here I am in my old clothes,
Riding on a pony,
A chicken feather in my hat,
And they call me "macaroni."

Macaroni! What is that?
A British slang for dandy!
Sure I'm not the best-dressed fellow,
But I'm mighty handy.

Yankee Doodle, let them laugh,
Those British in fine stitches.
We colonists can win the war
Without their fancy britches!

*May be sung to the tune of "Yankee Doodle"
(see also teacher's note 47).

Drums

What I like most
When the big parade comes
Is the *rat-a-tat rat-a-tat*
Marching drums.

I stand in the street
And I tap my feet
And I clap my hands
To the steady beat.

Rat-a-tat! They grow louder
And louder, then fade
As they pass me by
In the big parade.

I wish I could follow them
Rat-a-tat-tat!
I wish I could beat a drum
Just like that!

The Kettle Town Five

There were five young people, it's sad to say,
Who wanted and needed and had to play
Their musical instruments every which way
Twenty-four hours a day!

The first one's name was Annabelle.
She played the accordion very well.
She played for everyone in sight.
She played all day and she played all night
Until her father had to shout,
"Annabelle, you cut that out!"

The second was Thomas — Tom for short.
He played the trumpet very forte.
(That is, he blew it very loud.)
His father was extremely proud.
Tom blew all day and he blew all night
Till his mother lost her appetite.

The third was Donald, and he played the drum
With a *boom-boom-boom* and a *rum-tum-tum*.
He played with such a terrific beat,
You couldn't help but tap your feet.
But he played all night and he played all day,
And he drove the neighbors clean away.

The fourth one, Truman, had a slide trombone.
He couldn't leave that thing alone.
Back and forth, and forth and back —
He wouldn't even stop for a midnight snack.
Waa! Waa! Waa! he went,
Till the dogs howled, "Where's that instrument!"

The fifth and last was Antoinette.
She played the craziest clarinet.
She made her Kettle Town debut
With a *toodle-oodle-oodle-oo*.
But she toodled and oodled all night long,
Till even the cats cried, "Stop that song!"

"Go to bed!" said their fathers and mothers.
"Go to sleep!" said their sisters and brothers.
"I'm not tired. I want to jive!"
Said each of the terribly musical five.

What was Kettle Town going to do
With this constantly musical three plus two?
They wouldn't eat. They wouldn't sleep.
They played till they made the whole town weep.
Five different houses, five different tunes,
Mornings, evenings, afternoons!

"Make 'em march!" said the Kettle Town mayor.
"Maybe he's got something there,"
Said the Kettle Town folk.
This wasn't a joke.
"Why didn't I think of that before?"
Said the mayor, who had a surprise in store.

So the five came together.
They looked at each other.
"Let's hit it!" said Truman. "Let's go!" said Tom.
"There goes Annabelle!" shouted her mom.
"That's my Donald," said Donald's dad.
And Antoinette gave it all she had.

Toot toot toodle oo! Waa! Waa!
Rum tum! Rum tum! Blaa! Blaa!
There they go! They're the greatest group!
Diddly diddly boop-boop-a-doop!

The citizens cheered them up and down,
All over the streets of Kettle Town.
Our five were so tired when the day was done,
They slept on past the noonday sun.
They rested up for the next parade.
From that day on they really played.
They got it all together—the Kettle Town Five.
The Kettle Town citizens came alive.
But they also got to sleep at night.
Now everything's quite all right.

The String Family

Mama's a cello,
And Daddy's a bass.
Each of them sleeps
Inside a case.

They'll only come out
If you want to play,
And otherwise haven't
Got much to say.

Theirs is a family
That doesn't know
Anything lovelier
Than a bow.

You can tuck their children
Under your chin—
Sweet Viola
And Violin!

A Space Trip

I boarded a spaceship
One stormy day.
We shot toward the moon,
Which is not far away.

From there we decided
To go on to Mars,
And after our supper
We'd shoot for the stars.

But I started to think
Of my room and my bed
At home on the earth,
And I suddenly said—

"Do you think we could possibly
Turn this around?
I ought to go back
To solid ground.

"It's almost my bedtime.
I must get my sleep.
Tomorrow is school—
And appointments to keep."

The captain said, "Certainly.
If you insist."
And he brought me back home
Before I was missed.

It's a good thing, too,
Because—you see,
I forgot to tell Mom
Where I would be!

Moon

Sometimes silver, sometimes gold—
It looks like something I might hold.
Yet men have stood upon its face
And know that it's a different place—
Not a jewel for my hand,
But a distant mystery land.

On July 20, 1969, Neil Armstrong and Edwin "Buzz" Aldrin, Jr., were the first men to walk on the moon.

Star Pictures

When it's hot at night,
Grandma and I
Sit on the porch
And watch the sky.

She points her finger
Here and there
And tells me, "Look,
The Great Bear."

I try to see
How it can be
A bear, but it's
Just stars to me.

"Come on," says Grandma.
"There's his toes.
And there's his head,
And there's his nose."

I sit and stare,
And stare and stare,
And then I start
To see that bear!

Hear Me

I am the ocean.
Give me room!
I need to stretch myself out
from shore to shore.
I am the ocean.

Hear my sound.
Shhh. . .Shhh. . .
And *boom!*
And *roar!*
I am the ocean.
I am changeable.

I can creep up the sand so slowly,
you won't even notice me.
Yet I can crash over rocks and castles.
I can carry your buckets out to sea.
I am the ocean.
Look out for me.

I am deeper than deep.
I am greater than great.
Even my floor has mountains.
I am the ocean.
What more shall I say?

I am richer than rich
Plants and creatures (all sizes and shapes),

coral and seaweed,
barnacles, sharks, and whales,
shells, storms, and ships are mine.
What more shall I say?

I am the ocean.
I never rest.
I have energy and life.
I am constantly moving,
in and out, up and down,
around and around.
I am alive.
Hear my sound.

Calm,
gentle,
agitated,
strong—
All these I have been before.
You will never know me through and through,
though you explore, explore.

My secrets are deep.
I am the ocean.
I never sleep.
Shhh. . .Shhh. . .
I have secrets to keep.

The Octopus

The octopus
Is a very odd creature—
Eight arms are his
Most striking feature.

Tentacles
Those arms are called.
The octopus
Is thoroughly bald.

Here's something else
To make you think—
The octopus
Can squirt black ink.

But he can't write words—
He has no pen.
He can count to eight,
But never to ten.

He's not a puss
Like a pussy cat—
No, the octopus
Is nothing like that!

Whale and I

If I could sit on Whale's broad back,
I'd carry my lunch in a paper sack
And take a ride on the open sea—
If only Whale and I could agree.

He insists that I'd regret
Getting my jelly sandwich wet.
But I say (I don't mean to shout)
Why couldn't he turn off his spout?

Oyster

Oyster lives upon a rock.
This may come as an awful shock—
He has no nose, no ear, no eye.
His body's moist—it's never dry.
No brain in his even moister head,
He spends all day in his oyster bed!

What Do You Eat?*

Seal, Seal,
What do you eat?
    What do I eat?
    My favorite treat.
What is that? Bread and jam?
    Oh no, my favorite food is a clam.

Whale, Whale,
What do you eat?
    What do I eat?
    My favorite treat.
What is that? A vegetable dish?
    Oh no, my favorite food is a fish.

Shark, Shark,
What do you eat?
    What do I eat?
    My favorite treat.
What is that? Heaven forbid. . .
    Oh no, my favorite food is a squid.

*See teacher's note 48.

When the Tide Is Low

When the tide is low,
We look for shells—
Tiny pink bowls
And sand-colored bells—

Cones and conches
White as snow—
We pick them up
When the tide is low.

Laughing and shouting,
My sister grabs
At sand dollars
And little sand crabs.

She points at our footprints,
Sunk in the sand—
And touches the treasures
I hold in my hand.

There isn't a place
We'd rather go
Than down to the beach
When the tide is low.

AUGUST

Hot and Cold*

When you're cold
You think you'll freeze,
Think you'll freeze, think you'll freeze.
It helps if people
Hug and squeeze—
They're doing you a favor.

When you're hot
You moan and groan,
Moan and groan, moan and groan.
It helps to have
An ice-cream cone—
Any shape or flavor!

*May be sung to the tune of
"Mary Had A Little Lamb"

Tree House

Old boards for a floor
And a gunnysack wall—
No window or door,
No kitchen or hall—

It's half like a house
And half like a tent.
And we don't pay anybody
Five cents rent!

August Sawdust

August Sawdust was a boy
Who was always building stuff.
He sawed up wood and hammered nails—
He couldn't get enough.

He built a plane, he built a boat,
He built a racing car.
But no matter how he hammered and nailed,
They never went too far.

Then August Sawdust built a box—
He made it oh so neat.
And way down deep inside of it,
He placed a single seat.

He sat in it and sat until
Some kids came wandering by.
They couldn't imagine what it was
Or what it did or why—

But they never laughed—
They didn't dare.
August looked
So proud in there.

August wouldn't tell the kids
When they came to visit
What it was supposed to be,
Although they asked, "What *is* it?"

Whenever he sat inside that box,
His mind went miles an hour.
The fastest thing he'd ever built
Had *August Sawdust* power.

It didn't race, it didn't fly,
It didn't sail or sink.
It was August Sawdust's special box
In which to sit and *think*.

What do we call someone who builds with wood?

Have a Ball*

Crash! Bang! See those grins?
Down go ten unlucky pins.
Up they come. Now rolling, rolling —
Which ball is smooth and used for bowling?

Ping. . .Pong. . .Ping. . .Pong. . .
Which ball sings this song?
He isn't large. He isn't strong.
A table is where he'll belong.

Dribble, dribble. . .toss up high!
This ball is big, and you'll see why.
Do I even need to ask it?
What ball slips through an empty basket?

Crack goes the bat. The ball goes flying.
Somebody hit it, but it's not crying.
I can tell by your bright faces.
You know this ball — it goes with bases.

This ball's got points at either end.
You say you do not comprehend?
You're not really in a muddle.
Which ball can make eleven men huddle?

Eight wooden balls wait on the grass.
Through wire arches they must pass.
Smack them with mallets. Yes, you may.
It's only a game, you see — croquet!

Rubber and wood, pigskin and plastic,
Toss them, kick them — they're fantastic.
No two of them are quite the same.
Have a ball! Whatever your game!

*See teacher's note 49.

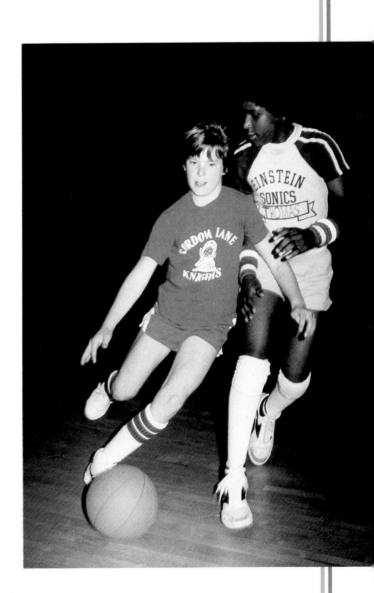

Hiking

Mountains grow
When people climb them—
The more we hike,
The higher they get.
My legs know it—
My feet know it.
But nobody else
Has discovered it yet!

*Do mountains really grow when you
climb them? Or do they just seem bigger?
Why?*

SSSSnake

How slithery slippery
Snake can be,
Crawling around
Without hand or knee—
Making *S*'s all over
With body and mouth—
His tail headed north
And his head headed south!

Squirrel

The scampering squirrel,
All fat and gray,
Is searching around
For acorns today.

There's one—he holds it
In his little front paws.
Will he eat it? No.
Not now. . .because. . .

He's going to find
A soft spot in the dirt
And bury it there—
Perhaps for dessert.

But if he forgets it,
That acorn will be
Growing to give us
A new oak tree!

The Doe in
the Meadow*

With her big ears,
The doe hears
The sounds of the meadow.
Noise makes her run
To the woods to hide
In the shadows.

When she returns,
If you're quiet
And gently greet her,
Maybe the doe
Will come and let you
Feed her!

*See teacher's note 50.

Fox in the Box

Max Fox
Got in a box,
And someone filled that box
With rocks.

What a fix
That fox was in.
He couldn't get out
To save his skin.

Some people arrived
To see the rocks.
They didn't know Max
Was in the box.

They dumped the rocks
Into some sacks,
And what do you know—
Out leaped Max!

A lady exclaimed,
"My goodness! Oh!
Did you see that fox?
He stepped on my toe!"

Max ran for a taxi—
Caught the Midnight Express.
And where did he go?
To Texas, I guess.

Evening on the Marsh

Above the soft land,
Above the tall grasses,
The great white swan
Silently passes.

In the shallow water
Tiny fish glide,
While the young frogs sing
On their lily-pad ride.

The quack of the ducks
And the cry of the loon
Announce the coming
Of the yellow moon.

The fireflies' lanterns
Glow in the night.
Now the great white swan
Can rest from her flight.

Mosquito

Long-legged needle-mouth,
How you bite!
Do you do it
Just for spite?
Hasn't anyone told you
It's impolite?

Dragonfly

Dragonfly
Patrols the stream.
She has got
A clever scheme
For catching Mosquito
And snatching Gnat—
That's how she gets
Her dragon fat!

Bats

When the sun goes down,
Bats wake from their sleep.
They begin to stir
And squeak and peep.

Then they dart about
Their cavernous room,
Anxious for
The deepening gloom.

They pour from their cave
Out into the night,
Huge black clouds
In hungry flight.

Gobbling beetles
And moths as they fly,
They darken the already
Darkened sky. . .

Only returning
When night grows gray
To hang from their ceilings
And sleep all day.

Scary Tales

In a cave in the ground
That was dark and gloomy,
Not a big cave,
Not very roomy—

Water dripping down
Through skinny cracks—
That kind of cave,
Where you can't relax—

We sat in the dark
And told scary tales,
And one of us started
To chew his nails—

And another one laughed
And another one cried.
Then we all jumped up
And ran outside.

The stars were shining—
And a pale half moon.
We said we'd come back—
But not too soon!

Echoes*

I threw my voice at the mountain
And the mountain threw it back
And back and back and back and back—
Along an airy track.

I threw my voice at the mountain
And it threw it back again
Again again again again—
I decided to keep it then.

Throw your voice at the mountain.
See what it will do
Will do will do will do will do—
It will throw it back to you!

What makes an echo?
*See teacher's note 51.

The Best Thing to Be

What is it like to be tall as a tree,
looking over the land and out to sea?

What is it like to be big as a whale,
riding the waves without engine or sail?

How would it feel to be small as a moth,
munching your way through the finest of cloth?

How would you like to be sweet as a pie. . .
red as an apple. . .blue as the sky?

Would you rather be different from what you are?
a lion? a daisy? a shooting star?

Something higher or wider. . .or older or new. . .
But why. . .when the best thing to be
is YOU!

Teacher's Notes

1 This poem can be used for helping the children get acquainted with one another. After you have read the poem and discussed it with the class, call for volunteers to be "shining faces" and give their names.

2 The discussion following the reading of this poem should ultimately lead to using the hands to signal; specifically, to signal in the classroom that one wants to speak.

3 Repeat this poem softly and rhythmically as the children are cutting. Vary the last lines as follows: Will you have a lot of shapes/When you get through? or You will have a lot of shapes/When you get through.

4 As you read the poem, pretend to be dipping a brush and painting—the brown low, the blue high, and so on. Ask questions such as these: What do you think I painted brown? (the ground) What do you think I painted blue? (the sky) Did you see any clouds in the sky? What did they look like? How would you paint them?

5 Be prepared to show pictures of any of these kinds of trees that do not grow in your area: pine trees, redwoods, weeping willows, various kinds of fruit trees. Before reading the poem, also present the idea of fairies as being little people, somewhat like Santa's elves.

6 After reading the poem, ask the children to tell what the last word of the poem was. (AWAY). Explain that you will read the poem again. This time, they are to listen very carefully and when you get to the last word, speak it with you. After the children have called out, "AWAY," ask, "What do we want to keep away?" They should respond , "DECAY."

7 This poem may be performed chorally, with one-half of the group reciting the first stanza, the other half reciting the second stanza, and everyone joining in to recite the last four lines.

8 Guide the children to identify the secret key as being imagination. Then allow ideas to flow freely as the children discuss the doors they would open and the things they would find.

9 This is fun for the children to sing as they march around the room in their Halloween costumes. Make a game of it in which a child must sit down if his or her costume is named. Finally "everyone else" sits down and only you (or a designated leader) is left standing.

10 Since there is usually a queen at Halloween, this is a good time to reinforce the sounds /kw/ spelled qu. The first stanza of the poem may also be used as an attention getter.

11 Use this poem as an exercise in observation skills. Use a variety of objects, allowing each to be seen for a limited time.

12 You may want to have an apple-tasting party in conjunction with this poem. Provide a variety of apples, plus a few other apple treats, for the children to taste. Let them experience not only tartness and sweetness but also various textures.

13 If you have the children sing this poem, let them sing the entire poem the first time. Then have them try the same thing, this time speaking the last two lines. Discuss which is more effective and why.

14 You may want to use this poem in a science lesson as an introduction to the concept of displacement of water.

15 This poem is to be read very rhythmically, with the children giving the answer to each question. You might then introduce a discussion of space travel. Ask what happens when the astronauts go up into space and why they don't fall back down.

16 This would be a good opportunity to show pictures of Christmas celebrations in different parts of the world. Help the children to understand that people are basically the same everywhere, even though they may look different in some ways, may dress differently, may eat different foods, and may have different customs.

17 This poem works well with a hand puppet.

18 This poem would make a good sign for a classroom workshop where the children can make gifts for family members and/or friends.

19 If you have Jewish children in your class, encourage them to tell the story of Hanukkah. Hanukkah commemorates the rededication of the Second Temple of Jerusalem after its desecration by the Syrian king Antiochus IV Epiphanes. It is celebrated for eight days, during which time candles are lighted in the multibranched candelabrum (menorah)—one the first night, two the second night, and so on. The ceremony recalls the Talmud story of how a small, one-day supply of oil that had escaped desecration continued to burn for eight full days until a new supply of consecrated oil could be obtained.

20 This poem provides a springboard for discussing opposites: summer-winter, hot-cold, wet-dry, and so on.

21 It's fun to substitute names of children in the class.

22 Use this poem as a workshop sign for a classroom post office. Do not limit the use of the post office to Valentine's Day. Encourage children to write letters to various people throughout the year.

23 In the discussion of this poem, introduce the word *frustrated.* It's a useful word for them to know. You may want to follow up the discussion by reading the next poem, "Being the Best You Can Be."

24 This poem might be retitled "The Shopping Center" or "The Mall," depending upon the area in which you live. After reading the poem, ask the children to identify "my favorite place." (the pet shop)

25 This poem is to be read rhythmically and may be accompanied by clapping and tapping. Before reading the poem, you might discuss the words *jockey, jasper* (a kind of quartz used for jewelry), *jade, jury,* and *judge.* As a follow-up to the poem, discuss the kinds of jobs family members hold. Then ask the children what kinds of jobs they think they would like to have.

26 You might also read this poem to the children as they swing on the playground swings.

27 Purim commemorates the survival of the Jews, who had been marked for death by their Persian rulers. The story is told in the Book of Esther. Haman, chief minister to King Ahasueras, was the

villain in the plot to massacre the Jews. When the Book of Esther is read during services on Purim, the congregation is expected to create a din. Gragers (noisemakers) are used. You can have the children make noisemakers by stapling together, mouth to mouth, two paper cups containing pebbles. The cups may be decorated with felt-tip marker or with cutouts.

28 Let the children create hats out of readily available materials. You may want to have them bring a variety of scraps and ornaments from home. Set aside a workshop area and use the poem as a workshop sign.

29 This holiday commemorates the "passing over" of the firstborn of the Jews when God "smote the land of Egypt" on the eve of the Exodus. The Jews had marked their doorposts so that the Angel of Death would know that they were the children of God. Because the Israelites had to leave Egypt hurriedly, they could not wait for bread to rise; hence, matzo, which is unleavened bread.

30 On a second reading, you might pause before the last word and allow the children to say, "Hoe."

31 As a follow-up activity, provide a variety of scents for children to sniff. You might also ask them to take their noses on a tour of the neighborhood (or a specific neighborhood that is convenient to reach). Have them prepare oral or written reports on the smells they found. Ideally, places like a bakery and a supermarket should be included on the tour. Also, if there is a road repair crew in the area using tar, this would be a good inclusion.

32 Before reading this poem, ask the children whether they can guess what kind of pet is purple and pink with spots and stripes and a tail you can see through. Allow them to guess for a time. Then read the poem.

33 After reading the poem, ask questions such as these: What did the girl's mother say? What did her father say? What did she get to have? If the children can't answer the questions, read the poem again and have the children listen to find the answers.

34 Toothpick people can be made, using flat toothpicks. Put dots for the eyes and nose and a line for a smile at the top of a toothpick. Draw a frown on the other side. When rolled back and forth between the fingers, the toothpick person will seem to change expression. Have the children make up a story about the toothpick family.

35 This would be a good opportunity to teach money values, using play money. Set up a "general store" in a workshop area of the room and use the poem as the workshop sign.

36 Ask children whether they know what a cud is. (The cow has two stomachs. A cow swallows its food without chewing and then brings it back up from the first stomach to chew. The regurgitated food is called a cud.) Ask whether the children know of any other animals that chew a cud. (goat, deer, antelope, giraffe, buffalo, camel, llama)

37 This would be a good opportunity to discuss automotive safety and the use of seat belts.

38 This poem can be used as an exercise. If you use it this way, you will need plenty of room for the children to move and an area to represent the lake. The children are to listen carefully and take steps only when you call out the numbers.

39 Discuss any words that may be unfamiliar. Read the poem. Ask the children to identify the sound they heard in many of the words in the poem. (/v/) Ask what letter stands for that sound. (v) Read the poem again and ask the children to listen carefully and to fill in the last word of each stanza. Point out that it rhymes with the last word in the second line.

40 Introduce the poem by asking whether any of the children have ever been on an airplane. Allow them to share their experiences briefly. Then ask them to close their eyes and imagine that they are going up in a plane. Let them describe how things below look as the plane goes higher and higher.

41 Encourage the children to do some "research." Let them talk with family members to determine their ethnic background and find out whether their names are different in the language of their forefathers. Some may be; some may not.

42 This is the kind of poem each line of which the children like to finish: One striped. . .(tiger), etc. Be sure the children understand what to ignore somebody means.

43 Ask the children to identify the animal described in each stanza of the poem: zebra, giraffe, elephant, kangaroo. You may want to explain that a baby kangaroo is called a joey (see the next poem).

44 This poem can be performed as an exercise. Have the children pair off facing each other. On each line they reach across to grab right hands, then left hands. The actions can also be performed with the children moving in a circle, square-dance fashion. Repeat as often as you wish, pausing between repeats.

45 Use as an exercise. Read the poem slowly and deliberately while the children move in a circle doing the elephant walk.

46 Clap hands over the head on each *BOOM*, then wiggle and dribble fingers down for the remainder of the lines to indicate fireworks bursting and sparks falling. In the last two lines, clap on every stress.

47 This is fun for the children to march to. The macaronis were a class of young English dandies of the late 18th and early 19th centuries who affected continental mannerisms.

48 Reread the poem, pausing before the final word of each stanza and allowing the children to supply the word: *clam, fish, squid,* respectively.

49 Have the children identify each unnamed game. Beginning with the second stanza, they are table tennis (Ping-Pong), basketball, baseball, and football.

50 This poem should be read very softly. It is almost an attention getter.

51 An echo is the repetition of sound caused by sound waves reflecting off surfaces. You might also want to introduce the Greek myth in which Echo was a beautiful nymph and a favorite of Diana, the goddess of the moon and of hunting. Echo had one failing; she loved to talk and insisted upon having the last word. One day, because Echo had angered her, Diana punished the nymph by taking away her ability to speak first. Echo would still have the last word—but only the last word.

Index of Titles

DEE LILLEGARD (Deanna Quintel) began writing poetry in San Leandro, California, at the age of nine. She has not stopped since. Ms. Lillegard's stories, poems, and puzzles have appeared in numerous publications and anthologies. Still á "California girl," she continues to write children's books and teaches writing for children.